A DISCIPLESHIP JOURNAL

MY ULTIMATE STORY

NexGen® is an imprint of
Cook Communications Ministries
Colorado Springs, CO 80918
Cook Communications, Paris, Ontario
Kingsway Communications, Eastbourne, England

MyUltimateStory
© 2007 by Empowerment Media

First Printing, 2007
Printed in the United States of America
2 3 4 5 6 7 8 9 10 Printing/Year 11 10 09 08 07

Written by Alison Simpson
Cover and Interior Design: studiogearbox.com
Photos: photos.com

ISBN 978-0-7814-4519-1

TABLE OF CONTENTS:

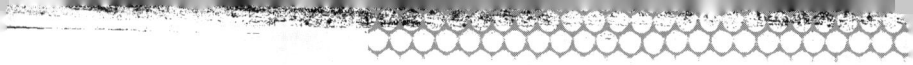

THINK: This section encourages you to take an intellectual journey into your own life, asking questions about your experiences and what the Bible has to say about them. You may be asked to remember events, read or analyze passages, fill out charts, or just ponder big questions.

LINK: These activities are relational, involving your personal connections with other Christ followers, mentors, and friends. Links might ask you to interview others, memorize Scripture together, ask questions, or participate in activities.

INK: This section presents a way to explore a principle in an inspiring or artistic way. No matter how creative you think you are (or aren't!), the Ink section presents an opportunity for imaginative expression, whether through music, visual art, technology, or writing.

HOW TO NAVIGATE YOUR ULTIMATE STORY

You will take many journeys in your lifetime. Some will be exhilarating; others will be mind-numbingly boring. Some will offer concrete answers; others will force you to ask questions. Some will bring risk and adventure; others will invite you to hold on to customs and traditions. **But no journey will be as significant as your journey toward Jesus Christ.**

This discipleship journal is designed as a five-week companion to the *Ultimate Choice* video series, and you'll want to bring it with you to youth group every week. It will guide you in taking an extreme step forward on your spiritual journey, but it won't be just another Sunday school lesson or sermon series. Its purpose is to encourage an exploration of Jesus Christ and his claims. Each week contains six daily missions. Each day presents three ways for you to explore God and your own story:

You probably won't complete all three tasks for every single day. And that's fine. The journal prompts are designed to inspire thought and promote a deeper understanding of yourself and your relationship with Jesus Christ. So jump into whatever task motivates you the most! Don't be afraid to experiment—and remember, sometimes the tasks that seem the hardest are the ones God can use to teach you the most.

Let's get started. It's time to write your *UltimateStory*!

WEEK ONE: GETTING STARTED

WHO IS THIS GOD OF THE BIBLE?

You're on the brink of an amazing journey. New challenges are stirring inside of you, and just like the cast members of *Ultimate Choice*, you're moving out on a great adventure.

Behind you is a land of doubt. What if God's only a mystical, cosmic force or a good-luck charm? Staring over your shoulder, you wonder if you should go back. The familiar landscape is all you've known, so why leave the territory?

You keep moving.

In front of you is a new land full of possibilities you haven't considered before. Its claims are risky: *Jesus Christ is the Son of God. The Bible is God's very message to humankind.* Exploring new territory is sometimes frightening. Are you ready to do it? You can't just read the tourist brochure. You've got to discover this place for yourself.

Life's most important journey requires some serious equipment. But you've already been given everything you need: a sharp intellect, an open heart, logical clarity, historical evidence, and a watertight road map.

Let's get after it.

My action plan for this week is . . .

DAY ONE

THINK

Everyone at church seems to think that the Bible is life's ultimate instruction manual—but you're not sure you buy it yet.

- What if some guys just made up a bunch of stuff a thousand years ago and claimed God told them to write it?
- Lots of people claim to have a holy book—what makes the Bible the right one?
- I've read so many verses in Sunday school . . . sometimes I get bored!

Without the Bible, all bets are off. If the Bible is wrong, man-made, flawed, or fake, then we might as well go home. If it's a book of fairy tales, we can't base our lives on its claims. And if it's just Sunday school filler, there's no reason to read it the rest of the week.

Honestly, no other book in history is better prepared to handle these skeptical questions. The Bible is a life-changing, utterly shocking, and superhuman message of hope and transformation. The short version of the Bible's defense looks like this:

- The historical manuscripts are unlike any other book.
- The archaeological connections have never lied.
- Multiple eyewitnesses have confirmed its truthfulness.
- Its predictions about the future are extraordinarily accurate.

Chances are good that you're not the first person to ask the questions you're asking now. But you've got to search the answers out for yourself. Where will you find them?

THINKING IT THROUGH

Write down at least five difficult questions you have about the Bible—its stories, the claims it makes, or the history behind it.

LINK

Think of the sturdiest, smartest, most trustworthy Christian you know. Guess what—he or she has likely been down the skeptic's road before. When deciding if something is worth believing in, a serious thinker will consider all the options and angles before saying, "Yeah, this is true."

Set up a face-to-face

DIGGING DEEPER

The answers to life's biggest questions can't be boxed in during a fifteen-minute devotional. Here are some of the best resources out there for answering them:

- *I Don't Have Enough Faith to Be an Atheist*, Geisler and Turek, 2004
- *Letters from a Skeptic*, Gregory A. Boyd, 2004
- *The Case for Faith* (Student Edition), Lee Strobel, 2002
- gotquestions.org
- ChristianityToday.com (look under the link, "Life & Faith" for Ignite Your Faith)

Spend some time digging for the answers to your biggest faith mysteries.

encounter with a mature Christian you trust. Ask him or her your tough questions. If you don't know what to ask, try these starter interview questions. Write down the responses you get. Add some more as your conversation deepens. Listen carefully.

Discussion on _____ with _____
(DATE)   (NAME)

When did you figure out that Christianity was really true and not just some empty religious exercise?

What were some of the questions about God you had when you were my age?

What has been one of the biggest "faith builders" of your lifetime?

INK

Eugene Peterson, in his preface to the book of Psalms in *The Message*, says this about prayer:

> *The impulse to pray is deep within us, at the very center of our created being. . . . Prayer is elemental, not advanced, language. It is the means by which our language becomes honest, true, and personal in response to God. It is the means by which we get everything in our lives out in the open before God.*[1]

As you begin to question, examine, and consider the evidence of the Bible and its claims, write an honest prayer to God. There is no wrong way to pray—no longings too surprising for him, no inquiries too difficult. Maybe start with an honest opener like "God, I just can't figure you out!" or "I hope you can hear me because I have so many questions."

You're not writing an essay. You're expressing your deepest soul-words to the God who made you! If you're a guy, remember: Prayers aren't just for girls or moms. If you think so, you haven't read many of David's prayers, which sometimes swell with anger or demand justice for his enemies.

When you finish, try reading your prayer out loud in a quiet room. God doesn't need to hear it (he knows it before it spills from your pen), but you will always find God's heart when you pray.

DAY TWO

THINK

Are you ready to go a little deeper?

Let's say the Bible is legitimate—the real deal. Its writers were faithful eyewitnesses to history, and the stories it tells really happened. The bigger question for you right now is, *who cares*? You're a regular guy or girl with modern problems, and you can hardly see how an ancient text can speak to your concerns.

But that's exactly why the Bible is so amazing. Even though it was written centuries ago, it's not tied to one culture or period in history. Its chapters are flavored with the sounds and smells of real life and specific people, but its principles are timeless. Moses, St. Augustine, Dietrich Bonhoeffer, and your best friend—they've all had different journeys and concerns, but the Bible has been relevant for each one.

Give that idea some more thought. Put a check mark by any topics that are relevant to your life. If it's a biggie on your list, put a plus sign next to it.

sexuality	the future	loneliness
money	politics	anger
depression	love	marriage
parties	enemies	fear
drunkenness	desire	
relationships	war	

What are some other topics that feel relevant to you at this stage of life?

From your past experience or study, what do you think the Bible says about these topics? Is that a guess—or do you have some firm idea? Just be honest.

LINK

Grab a friend. When the cast members get together during *Ultimate Choice*, they're able to share common experience and insights. Find a common thread with a trusted buddy—maybe a shared doubt or pressing question—and prowl around the Bible's pages looking for some insight together. You might not find a "magic verse" to print on a T-shirt, but you will discover that God cares deeply about your everyday concerns.

DIGGING DEEPER

So what does God's story have to do with your story? If you've only studied your Bible the old-fashioned way, try a new method. Go to BibleResources.Bible.com and use their "keyword search" link. Type in one of your topics like the *future* or *marriage*, and zip . . . you've got a wealth of Scripture that connects you with God's principles.

A cautionary word: The "answer hunter" approach sometimes leaves out important context clues. Make sure you don't isolate a verse you like and forget to figure out the big picture of what the writer was talking about.

Topic #1:

_____

What Does the Bible Have to Say about It?

Topic #2:

_____

What Does the Bible Have to Say about It?

Topic #3:

_____

What Does the Bible Have to Say about It?

INK

Get your hands on Sara Groves' song "The Word" from her album *Conversations*. Download the lyrics from a Christian music Web site and check out her insights about modern life and the Bible.

DAY THREE

THINK

The centerpiece of God's story is Jesus Christ.

Other groups claim their own favorite prophets, storytellers, mystical spirits, or scientific theories. But Jesus stands taller than the rest—and for very good reason. Unlike other wise leaders or rebellious revolutionaries, Jesus Christ did things that no man could do. Want proof? Take a look:

- All of the predictions about him were true and accurate.
- He performed unprecedented miracles confirmed by many eyewitnesses.
- He was raised from the dead.

Respond to each of the following:
- I'm afraid Genesis doesn't fit with what I'm being taught in science class. Just because the Bible doesn't contain all of the scientific facts, does that mean it's false?
- Despite the evidence, a lot of people would rather believe that Jesus was just an ordinary man; that way, it's easier to dismiss the powerful things he taught.

· The resurrection makes all the difference in the world. If the disciples knew that Jesus had not been raised from the dead, he would have been exposed as a fraud. Why would they have died for the cause of Christ if they knew he was a fake?

What do you think?

DIGGING DEEPER

You need more than a day to wrap your head and heart around the astonishing truth of who Jesus is and what his life means for you.

Check out these great resources for exploring Jesus Christ.

- *The Case for Christ*, Lee Strobel, 1998
- *No Wonder They Call Him the Savior*, Max Lucado, 2004
- *Seeing and Savoring Jesus Christ*, John Piper, 2004
- *Why Jesus Matters*, Bruce Bickel and Stan Jantz, 2003

LINK

Remember in the video when the cast members were strapped to the backs of their skydiving partners? Like them, you're not alone in this walk of faith. Here's an idea that will give you courage.

As you begin to gather more evidence of Jesus Christ's divine nature, you might need a little practice "giving an answer" to those who ask, "What's up with the Jesus guy any-way?" Practice the art of *apologetics*—a fancy word that simply means being able to defend your beliefs.

How should you practice? Find a Christian friend and chat about the questions skeptics like to toss out. If face-to-face practice is hard to fit into your schedule, blogging or IMing can work as well. Besides giving you some valuable practice at explaining your faith, you might even go deeper than ever in your friendship.

INK

We often hear of people writing letters to God, but have you ever writ-ten a letter to Jesus?

What makes this exercise so important is that when you write to Jesus, you are composing a letter to a *person*. Not a cosmic Santa, not the "force" in *Star Wars*, but a real man whose hunger pangs and cal-loused feet were just like ours.

Your letter will tell a lot about your relationship with him. Will it be awkward and embarrassed? Will you share openly, as you would with a loyal friend? Perhaps it will bear the mark of a love letter, unashamed-ly intimate and honest. You may find it easier to let your letter take the shape of a prayer.

Whatever form it takes, let it teach you something about his very nature.

DAY FOUR

THINK

You're getting to know Jesus more and more. Put a word or phrase that describes him in each box on the left. On the right, fill in some words or phrases that don't describe him.

Jesus Christ IS . . .	Jesus Christ is NOT . . .
God's Son	Imaginary
My role model	Scary

LINK

Prayer is sometimes silent and meditative, but it's also to be shared with others. When is the last time you initiated prayer time with another Christian? Not just at the dinner table or during youth group, but a scheduled time of prayer with a friend?

Be brave and link up with someone else—even a small group of three or four—and pray for each other. If you don't know how or you feel uncomfortable, that's okay. Just start somewhere. Consider reading the prayers in the book of Psalms out loud, or have each person bring a written prayer to share.

INK

A writer once committed herself to writing daily in a journal because, as she said, "I've already forgotten many of the people I used to be." You may think you will always remember who you are today, but just wait… stages start to melt together and sometimes life lessons are forgotten.

If you haven't already started a journal, you should. It doesn't matter the size or shape. Grab a beautiful blank book or a ratty spiral notebook and take a risk. Or log onto Xanga, Blogspot, or another online source. The format doesn't matter—it's the content that will capture your journey.

WARNING:

Remember that online journals are visible to lots of people—even those you don't know. So be careful not to share information that would help strangers find you in person. Be smart and utilize Internet safety features that will allow only your friends and family to read your deep thoughts. Finally, talk to your parents about online journaling; get their support before you begin.

If you think diaries are only for kids, forget what you've imagined about that. Writing in a journal is much more than listing your day's events or rambling about any old thing. It's a place to dump what's floating around—or flying around—in your mind and heart.

If it's your first attempt at a journal, try this for an opening page:

The Life and Adventures of:

Age:

Started on:

Write your favorite verse or quote to record this stage of your life.

DAY FIVE

THINK

As your journey picks up speed, the evidence for the truth of the Bible will make a bigger and bigger pile. But is evidence the same as faith? At some point, you will need to go beyond the facts about God into the land of spiritual transformation.

According to influential Christian writer and thinker Norman Geisler, people face more than just rational obstacles when it comes to faith in Jesus Christ.[2] Number one is the *emotional* barrier. Your uncle's loud, obnoxious prayers, your brother's holier-than-thou attitude, a bad experience with another Christian—all of these can be barriers to accepting the truth of God's Word. Sometimes we just don't do a good job separating God's voice from our own interpretations. But you can't throw God out just because his so-called followers mess up or make you uncomfortable.

Write down at least five emotional barriers that have kept you from really grabbing onto God:

This kind of honesty isn't easy. It forces us to face ugly, difficult, troubling situations, and learn to find God in spite of them—sometimes even because of them.

DIGGING DEEPER

It's time for you to get into the truth about God. You need to know his personality so clearly that you see him even when others' behavior might camouflage his character.

How can you do this? Well, you start by studying his traits.

Using the online method you used on Day Two, try studying the character of God using the key words below to guide your study. You can even try different translations, such as the *New American Standard Version* or *The Message*, to see how his traits are expressed in different language styles.

HOLY: Look up "holy" and "holiness" in the BibleResources.Bible.com/ search. You can write down entire verses, Scripture references (the book, chapter, and verse numbers), or just phrases where you find them.
What do you think this means?
Where do you find evidence in the Bible that God is holy?

UNCHANGING: Look up "unchanging" and "immutable."
Is this a trait we can share with God? Why or why not?
What verses or phrases address this attribute?

WISE: Look up "wise" and "wisdom."
How do you think God's wisdom is different from ours?

LOVING: Your search will turn up a bazillion love phrases, but narrow your search to "God's love" and you'll get a more specific view.
This one seems too easy, but is it? What do you think separates God's love from ours?

LINK

It's been said that the biggest barrier to Christianity is often Christians themselves. How can you minimize your frustration with other people and their sometimes stupid behavior?

The book of Romans treats this subject with delicacy and grace. Read the following section over many times, turning it over in your mind—even memorizing parts of it! **In the margins or directly in the passage, write notes or circle phrases that carry a lot of meaning for you.**

Welcome with open arms fellow believers who don't see things the way you do. And don't jump all over them every time they do or say something you don't agree with—even when it seems that they are strong on opinions but weak in the faith department. Remember, they have their own history to deal with. Treat them gently.

For instance, a person who has been around for a while might well be convinced that he can eat anything on the table, while another, with a different background, might assume he should only be a vegetarian and eat accordingly. But since both are guests at Christ's table, wouldn't it be terribly rude if they fell to criticizing what the other ate or didn't eat? God, after all, invited them both to the table. Do you have any business crossing people off the guest list or interfering with God's welcome? If there are corrections to be made or manners to be learned, God can handle that without your help.

Or, say, one person thinks that some days should be set aside as holy and another thinks that each day is pretty much like any other. There are good reasons either way. So, each person is free to follow the convictions of conscience.

What's important in all this is that if you keep a holy day, keep it for God's sake; if you eat meat, eat it to the glory of God and thank God for prime rib; if you're a vegetarian, eat vegetables to the glory of God and thank God for broccoli. None of us are permitted to insist on our own way in these matters. It's God we are answerable to—all the way from life to death and everything in between—not each other. That's why Jesus lived and died and then lived again: so that he could be our Master across the entire range of life and death, and free us from the petty tyrannies of each other.

So where does that leave you when you criticize a brother? And where does that leave you when you condescend to a sister? I'd say it leaves you looking pretty silly—or worse. Eventually, we're all going to end up kneeling side by side in the place of judgment, facing God. Your critical and condescending ways aren't going to improve your position there one bit. Read it for yourself in Scripture:

"As I live and breathe," God says,
    "every knee will bow before me;
Every tongue will tell the honest truth
    that I and only I am God."

So tend to your knitting. You've got your hands full just taking care of your own life before God.

—ROMANS 14:1–12

INK

You know those emotional barriers you identified earlier? The ones that have kept you from embracing God? They may be very real, but that doesn't mean they're healthy. In fact, there are no good excuses for creating distance between yourself and God. **Spend some time writing about those barriers in more detail. What happened that caused you to pull away from God? What can you do to restore trust and fellowship?**

DAY SIX

THINK

You've managed to work through some of your intellectual obstacles, and you've explored your emotional ones. But there might be one more thing standing between you and the new land God wants to show you.

Fear.

On *Ultimate Choice*, Donovan shared about his fears of facing the unknown. Maybe you fear that God will ask you to do something uncomfortable, unpopular, or uncool. Or maybe you're afraid that the Bible's claims are too radical. There's also the fear of letting go of familiar territory and safe patterns of belief and behavior.

Sorry to break this to you, but God does ask us to be uncomfortable, uncool, and sometimes unpopular. His claims *are* radical. Yes, you're on the brink of leaving familiar territory and safe customs of behavior. That is all true.

But the fabulous, life-changing, and almost unbelievable part of the story is that God's intentions spring from his love, and "perfect love drives out fear" (1 John 4:18 NIV). The Bible is the love story about God and his people. We are not asked to leave our homeland at the stern order of a distant king or dictator. We are asked to join him on a journey of infinite adventure. He is a leader without fault. He is a leader who loves you.

This sort of love is not normal. It does not follow rules of logic—*you scratch my back; I'll scratch yours!* God's love is unfailing, unconditional, and completely free. Can something free cost us? It will cost you your own road map, your own notions of success, your own hunt for meaning. But only in giving those up will you find the real road home.

What are you most afraid of about the future?

LINK

No life-changing experience should stay secret for very long. How are you going to share this amazing journey?

Those closest to you need to know where you're headed. Your family needs to know—and you should be prepared for anything. Maybe your parents will be thrilled because they've been praying for your journey for quite some time. Or maybe they'll be skeptical of your new enthusiasm. Some friends will have questions, and still others will try to talk you out of this wild ride.

(continued on page 28) ➔ ➔ ➔

DIGGING DEEPER

What does God say are the requirements for following him? Check out these verses:

The king stood by his pillar and before GOD solemnly committed himself to the covenant: to follow GOD believingly and obediently; to follow his instructions, heart and soul, on what to believe and do; to confirm with his life the entire covenant, all that was written in the book.
—2 Chronicles 34:31

Then he told them what they could expect for themselves: "Anyone who intends to come with me has to let me lead. You're not in the driver's seat—I am. Don't run from suffering; embrace it. Follow me and I'll show you how. Self-help is no help at all. Self-sacrifice is the way, *my* way, to finding yourself, your true self. What good would it do to get everything you want and lose you, the real you?"
—Luke 9:23–25

One day when large groups of people were walking along with him, Jesus turned and told them, "Anyone who comes to me but refuses to let go of father, mother, spouse, children, brothers, sisters—yes, even one's own self!—can't be my disciple. Anyone who won't shoulder his own cross and follow behind me can't be my disciple."
—Luke 14:25-27

What might God be asking *you* to do?

You need to be ready to share your heart, but how can you pre-pare? One good way is to write a letter, composing your thoughts and ideas ahead of time. Consider these important words when you write: *respect, passion,* and *sincerity*. Your closest allies will rejoice with you when they see that your enthusiasm is authentic.

INK

Nichole Nordeman sings a song entitled "Brave" from the same-named CD that may well become your motto for this week. Download the lyrics, print them out, and post them somewhere.

Like any great poem, it takes ordinary words like *fire, storm,* and *gate* and makes them symbols for more meaningful things. **What do you think they mean for your life? What does the term *status quo* mean?** Get that song moving in your head, put it in your permanent music collection, and be brave!

WEEK TWO: GETTING STARTED

WHY SHOULD I OBEY GOD?

God's been called every name on the planet: a force, an entity, a supreme being. Some say he created the world and then left town; others claim he's actually part of the leaves and flowers.

Doesn't seem very personal, huh? When we have that picture of God, it's no wonder obedience doesn't sound exciting. Think about it—an impersonal force goes around making up rules for people to follow. No thanks!

God says this: *"I want you to show love, not offer sacrifices. I want you to know me more than I want burnt offerings"* (Hosea 6:6 NLT). When you know that the God of the universe wants a relationship with *you*, obedience becomes more than just rule following. It's a loving response to your Creator.

My action plan for this week is . . .

DAY ONE

THINK

What do these quotations say about the personal love of God? In the spaces after each quote, try to restate them in your own words.

> God is not a cruel slave driver or a bully who uses brute force to coerce us into submission. He doesn't try to break our will, but woos us to himself so that we might offer ourselves freely to him. God is a lover and a liberator, and surrendering to him brings freedom, not bondage. [3]

> The love of Christ is beyond all knowledge, beyond anything we can intellectualize or imagine. It is not mild [goodness] but a consuming fire. Jesus is so unbearably forgiving, so infinitely patient and so unendingly loving that he provides us with the resources we need to live lives of gracious response. [4]

LINK

Take a poll at school or some social event—anywhere you're likely to get a variety of opinions. Ask different kinds of people these questions and see what answers you get.

How would you define God?

What do you think God looks like?

What are three words that describe God?

When you listen to people's answers, don't interrupt or judge them. Write them down and be respectful. Loving dialogue can open up people's interest about the authentic God of the Bible.

INK

DIGGING DEEPER

What are some of the false ways we define the character of God?

Some people portray God as____
_____.

In the past, I've thought that God was a lot like_____
_____.

Test these opinions against the Bible. What's the truth about God?

Some verses to get you started:

- God Is Powerful: Genesis 18:14, Deuteronomy 32:39, 2 Chronicles 20:6, Luke 1:37, Luke 18:27, Revelation 19:6

- God Never Changes: Numbers 23:19, Psalm 89:34, Psalm 102:24-27, Romans 11:29, Hebrews 6:13-20

- God Is Righteous and Just: Genesis 18:25, Psalm 11:7, Psalm 119:142, 1 John 1:5, Revelation 15:3, Revelation 16:4-7

Sometimes the Bible uses metaphors to illustrate God's love for us. For example, God says in Isaiah that he has *branded* us on the palms of his hands; Paul was eager to call himself a *bondservant* of Christ; and, in the Psalms, we are precious *lambs* cared for by our Good Shepherd.

Can you draw a picture of it? Or write a song about it? Compose a poem? Use the following questions to guide your inspiration.

DIGGING DEEPER

When I think of God's love, it reminds me of

_____.

If God's love were an object, it would be

_____ ___.

DAY TWO

THINK

Hundreds of years ago, a guy named Machiavelli said that if you want to control people, it is better to be feared than loved.

Do you agree?
What is the difference between obeying God's standards because you love him and obeying only because you fear him?

LINK

Sometimes the way our parents view obedience can prompt some questions about obeying God. Here is an exercise for you and your parents to do together. Be careful: You might learn a lot about each other!

Put a dot in the spot that best represents your answer. Your dot might end up closer to one of the sides or in the middle. *Don't look at each other's answers until you've both decided where to put your dots.*

When you're done, talk about your answers. How does your relationship with your parents affect how you view God?

For the son or daughter:

How obedient am I?

perfectly compliant ....completely rebellious

How strict are my parents?

totally strict...completely lenient

What motivates me?

love ....fear

For Mom or Dad:

How obedient is my child?

perfectly compliant ....completely rebellious

How strict am I as a parent

totally strict...completely lenient

What do I use to motivate my child?

love ....fear

INK

It's time to get *way* ahead of yourself. Imagine that you are a parent of a teenager just like you. You have the task of teaching her right from wrong, and helping her stay out of trouble.

In your journal, write down your "parenting strategy" in three columns:

What do I want to teach my child?	How am I going to teach it?	What issues am I willing to compromise on?

DIGGING DEEPER

Read this passage:

> God can do anything, you know—far more than you could ever imagine or guess or request in your wildest dreams! He does it not by pushing us around but by working within us, his Spirit deeply and gently within us. —Ephesians 3:20

How do you think this concept works in your own life?

DAY THREE

THINK

These days, when it comes to morality, it seems like everybody makes up his own set of rules. But how do you know whether a rule is a God-rule or just somebody's opinion?

Look at the chart below. On the left, write down some rules that you believe are things the Bible commands us to follow. On the right side, list some rules you think are people's personal opinions.

God-rules

Example: Don't have sex before you're married.

Man-made rules

Example: Get straight A's this year in school.

LINK

On the show, Jesse and Jeremiah worried they'd end up compromising their values to fit in with their friends. In the privacy of this journal, write your name in the center circle below. Then, write down the names of your friends and acquaintances. Place the names of the people who share your values closest to your name. Farther away, write the names of the friends whose values differ from yours.

AN IMPORTANT NOTE:

This exercise should be private; its purpose is not to judge your friends, but to examine for yourself the "inner circle" of support you've chosen. Use code names if you suspect someone will see this journal.

DIGGING DEEPER

How would you define the word *conscience*?

Do you think your conscience is reliable?

Can you find a passage in the Bible that speaks about your conscience?

Now for a hard question! Are you using your friends' standards to judge your own behavior? In other words, is your goal just to be better behaved than your friends? Or are you measuring yourself against God's standards?

The thing about God's standards is they don't change with the circumstances of your life. Morality doesn't depend on who your friends are or how you measure up against them, your siblings, or even your parents. It's all about you living in close relationship with God and following *his* directions.

INK

You are surrounded every day by messages, some encouraging you to live by God-rules and others persuading you to live by man-made ones. Turn on the TV, pop in your headphones, or glance at the billboards on your way to school, and you can't help but be bombarded by these messages.

Take a few minutes today to evaluate what kind of messages you're letting into your head (and your heart). Look through your CD collection or scroll through your iPod. What is each song saying? Does it bring you closer to God or hold up the world's standards? We're not asking you to go on a "throw away all your CDs" rampage (though you might find yourself doing just that). Just listen to the lyrics, take a look at Scriptures, and let God do the rest.

DAY FOUR

THINK

Yesterday, you tried to see the difference between God's standards—which are fixed and unchanging—and human opinion, which twists and shapes the rules to fit our desires.

Think about times when you've twisted firm principles to get a short-term payoff. (Be honest—God already knows about it anyway!) Write down God's standard in the first column, then compare it to your own standards in the second column.

Remember the game where your team was trying to decide which Frisbee to keep and which one to toss back? God's standards aren't that mysterious, although we like to complicate them. As DJ reminded us in the video, some people are so tempted by an immediate thrill that they lose perspective on the unchanging standards of God.

God's Principle Says . . .   **But I Justified It By . . .**

Example: Be modest with my ⟶ Saying that the shirt was the latest clothing. (1 Timothy 2:9)   style.

⟶

⟶

⟶

⟶

LINK

Some of God's standards are easy to follow, but others may pose a life-long challenge. God gives us plenty of defenses (the Holy Spirit, our conscience, forgiveness from sin), but he also expects us to stay accountable to each other.

Create an accountability group with people you trust. A group like this should give you a safe place to share your struggles and should hold you responsible when you fall. Group members can be mature teens, trusted adults, or a mixture of the two.

God wants us to cultivate honesty:

". . . no more lies, no more pretense. Tell your neighbor the truth. In Christ's body we're all connected to each other, after all. When you lie to others, you end up lying to yourself."

—EPHESIANS 4:25

INK

(For Girls)

Take different colors of string or leather—one for each member of your group—and braid them together into bracelets. Make enough for each person to wear one, and use them as reminders to pray for and encourage each other.

(For Guys)

Write down the names of your group members on half a dozen sticky notes. Post them in prominent places—the car visor, your bathroom mirror, your computer monitor—as a reminder to pray for each other during the week.

DAY FIVE

THINK

Some are big. Some are small. What risks are worth taking? Which ones are just short-term thrills?

LINK

Jeremiah chapter two explains the problem the nation of Israel had with being faithful to God. They started out as loving as a young bride, and they ended up betraying God and becoming as unfaithful as a prostitute. Even worse, God says they were like animals in heat—hooking up with anyone and everyone:

You are like a wild donkey, sniffing the wind at mating time. Who can restrain her lust? Those who desire her don't need to search, for she goes running to them! When will you stop running? When will you stop panting after other gods? But you say, "Save your breath. I'm in love with these foreign gods, and I can't stop loving them now!"

(VV. 24–25 NLT)

THINKING IT THROUGH

And so I insist—and God backs me up on this—that there be no going along with the crowd, the empty-headed, mindless crowd. They've refused for so long to deal with God that they've lost touch not only with God but with reality itself. They can't think straight anymore. Feeling no pain, they let themselves go in sexual obsession, addicted to every sort of perversion. — Ephesians 4:17–19

So what do "foreign gods" have to do with you? Today, these idols are all the risks and thrills that draw us away from our one true source. Anything we use to find fulfillment apart from the one true God is a foreign god. And there are always costs involved in chasing them.

Find a trusted adult to interview about the price he or she has had to pay for disobedience. (The questions are very personal—and not always easy to answer—so let your partner know ahead of time the kinds of questions you will be asking.)

DIGGING DEEPER

Check out John Bunyan's classic book *The Pilgrim's Progress*. It's what we call an allegory—a story that uses objects, places, and symbols to represent more meaningful things.

The lead character (appropriately named Christian) has to journey past all kinds of obstacles—cheap thrills, lust, pride, anger, you name it—before he gets to the Celestial City.

How is life more of an adventure when we conquer these booby traps than when we get stuck in them?

DAY SIX

THINK

On *Ultimate Choice,* Jason realized that his selfish decisions had consequences for other people. Have you ever had a revelation like that?

We are designed for human connection, and our families, peers, and community affect us, just as we affect them. Sometimes this is good, and sometimes it's bad.

When you're surrounded by negative influences, well-meaning Christians might say, "Believe in yourself. Be strong and know who you are. Be secure enough to say no." These are simple answers—you even heard some of them on the show—but they are more easily said than done, given our need to be accepted, loved, and desired by others.

LINK

If stress and social expectations are making you crazy, examine yourself. What ideas are you putting into your mind that makes the pressure worse? For example, the more you watch TV and movies, the more you compare yourself with the characters you see on the screen. The more you read magazines, hang out with shallow friends, or buy into the myth of celebrity glitter, the more your mind gets twisted into the shape of the culture.

DIGGING DEEPER

It's important to remember that God hasn't left you alone in the decision-making process. He has given you wise instruction on how to grow strong. And he has promised to do his special work to transform you and help you. Look up the following verses and summarize what they tell you. Then you'll have an encouraging reminder of how you can grow the spiritual muscles for sticking to God's standards.

MY PART

Colossians 2:6-7

Ephesians 4:22–24

Proverbs 4:23

Psalm 119:97

GOD'S PART

2 Corinthians 3:18

1 Corinthians 2:12

Acts 20:32

1 Corinthians 10:13

Pick a friend and do this together: Create an inventory of some of the shows, movies, songs, or magazines you've been exposed to in the last six months. Write down the following information about each one:

Title	Characters' Actions	Characters' Values	What would God say about it?

INK

Even younger kids recognize the difficulty of making right decisions when everyone else is moving in another direction. Write a script for a short play or a puppet show illustrating the differences between good and bad choices. Ask your children's director or pastor if you can share your production during a Sunday school or children's event.

WEEK THREE: GETTING STARTED

WHO'S BEHIND THE WHEEL?

Who's steering your life? How can you really know that God's a better driver than you are? Even after you're convinced of it, how can you "let go" without everything unraveling?

Driving a car is an excellent metaphor for our lives. Every kid who's ever attended driver's training has heard the lecture: *This isn't a bumper-car ride or video game—this is the real deal! If you think it's only fun and games, you're not ready for the road.*

Your Driver's Ed teacher is right. When you take the wheel of a car, you have to accept the responsibilities that go along with it. And guess what—life has way more risks than driving. That's why we need help!

Letting go of control is always scary. The real question is *who is better equipped to run my life—me or God?* Letting go gives God an opportunity to show up in power!

My action plan for this week is . . .

DAY ONE

THINK

Americans are famous for thinking we're the makers of our own destiny. But how much of this is an illusion? Let's see how much of your life you believe you control. On one side, write down some things you have no control over. On the other side, write down examples of things you *can* control.

I Have No Control

Example: My parents' relationship

I'm in Control

Example: My grades at school

Now, write about some moments when you thought your world was disordered and chaotic, but then realized that God was in control all along. How did you come to realize he was in charge?

LINK

One way we can learn to take our hands off the joystick of our lives and turn it over to God is to actively remember his goodness and faithfulness. The more we are aware of God's perfect power, the easier it will be to trust him.

One way you can *actively remember* is to tell others stories of how God has shown up in your life. This week, look for one opportunity to tell a friend or family member about a time when things felt out of control and God came through in a real way.

DIGGING DEEPER

Do you struggle with wanting to control everything? God has asked us to use our free will to serve him, but we must also accept that some things are beyond our control. If we trust God to know what he's doing, then we will be able to accept even heavy disappointments that knock us off our feet.

He is faithful: *The one who calls you is faithful and he will do it.* —1 Thessalonians 5:24 NIV

He is loving: *If you brag, brag of this and this only: That you understand and know me. I'm GOD, and I act in loyal love. I do what's right and set things right and fair, and delight in those who do the same things. These are my trademarks.* —Jeremiah 9:24

He is just: *GOD makes everything come out right; he puts victims back on their feet.* —Psalm 103:6

He knows what he's doing: *So if you find life difficult because you're doing what God said, take it in stride. Trust him. He knows what he's doing, and he'll keep on doing it.* —1 Peter 4:19

INK

Recording the adventures in your life is an important step to recognizing God's hand at work. **Write the story of your week below. As you do so, consider the following things: How did God intervene in my week? When did I see evidence of his goodness? How do I know he's looking out for my best interest?**

DAY TWO

THINK

Have you ever felt wiped out, pushed back, unraveled, or knocked flat? Setbacks come for two reasons: because of sin and disobedience, or because of limitations we can't change. Neither one feels good. On *Ultimate Choice,* Jason's setbacks in the river happened not because of any sin but because of currents he couldn't control. Donovan, on the other hand, faced setbacks stemming from lifestyle choices he made.

The good news is that God can use both kinds of setbacks to accomplish something good!

God does this in ways we can't even wrap our minds around. He ties together unraveled threads at the speed of light, and most of the time we don't even see his hand at work. Behind the scenes, God is in charge whether you can see it or not.

Below are some examples of setbacks that require you to take action and some that require you to "let go and let God." Circle the ones that apply to your life.

LET GO

divorce in the family

difficult or rebellious sibling

physical handicap

family financial struggles

death of a loved one

an absent parent

painful memories

chronic illness

personality traits

genetic limitations

an overbearing parent

bullying by others

emotional scars

physical limitations

other: _____

TAKE ACTION

risky behavior

ditching school

laziness

addiction to video games

binge drinking

bad attitude or heavy sarcasm

sexual experimentation

fighting with peers

disobeying parents

pornography

God-dishonoring media

disrespecting authority

breaking the law

lying

other: _____

Can you see the difference? Sometimes God wants us to release control, and other times he wants us to take action. God gives strength in both circumstances. **Write about some of the situations you circled, or add some of your own.**

LINK

If you circled quite a few items in the "Let Go" section, you may need extra help. Ask your mom or dad to schedule an appointment with a professional Christian counselor who is especially trained to help you get past some of life's deepest pain. There is no shame in getting help; sometimes the adults in your life may not even know what struggles are going on inside you. Reach out!

INK

The concept of *letting go* is always harder than it seems. One way to give weight to something so abstract is to follow up a decision with a symbolic gesture.

Take a look at your "Let Go" list for today. If something is really painful or difficult, try writing it down, putting it in a box, and burying it somewhere. Yeah, that's right—*bury it.* Get an old box, write down all the things you know you can't control, and seal it up! Don't put it in the backyard as a constant reminder, but take it to a place where you won't be tempted to look at it again.

God wants to take you to new places, and letting go will help you travel light!

DAY THREE

THINK

Do you think God only uses strong people? Does he only use the pretty, clever girls or cool, smooth guys? No way! In the Bible, God uses all kinds of people—usually the ones we would least expect to get the assignment.

The Bible is full of surprising paradoxes—things that at first don't make sense. For example, "When I am weak,

DIGGING DEEPER

Check out these Bible stories:

- Choosing Moses—Exodus 3
- The Blinding of Saul—Acts 9
- John the Baptist—John 1

How do these stories illustrate the paradox of strength in weakness?

then I am strong" (2 Corinthians 12:10 NIV). Doesn't add up, does it? But like other mysteries in the Bible, we see this played out in our own lives, so we know it's true.

Ultimate Choice uses a river as its backdrop for this week's session. It's a perfect metaphor, really, with its powerful current and overwhelming strength. The rafting instructor tells the participants to resist the urge to stand up in the current, but instead relinquish control. That hardly seems like good advice! But in God's world, it's often a requirement.

Read the following passage from Louie Giglio's book: *I Am Not But I Know I AM:*

> *God is always looking for ordinary people to play significant roles in his unfolding story. And, given that he is God and supremely confident in himself, he is free to choose the least among us—the slowest, the lesser known, the last, the smallest, the poorest—to accomplish amazing, God-sized stuff.*[5]

How does this paradox work in your life? Think about how God has used your weaknesses to do big things. Write about a time when God took something ordinary and created a God-sized result.

LINK

Your community is filled with people who have struggled with many of the same things you have. Do you know someone whose life demonstrates the principle of strength in weakness? Write him or her a letter of encouragement or admiration.

DIGGING DEEPER

Look at these three different translations of 2 Corinthians 12:9–10. Circle words and phrases that illustrate the paradox of strength within weakness.

The he told me, My grace is enough; it's all you need. My strength comes into its own in your weakness. Once I heard that, I was glad to let it happen. I quit focusing on the handicap and began appreciating the gift. It was a case of Christ's strength moving in on my weakness. Now I take limitations in stride, and with good cheer, these limitations that cut me down to size—abuse, accidents, opposition, bad breaks. I just let Christ take over! And so the weaker I get, the stronger I become. (MSG)

But he said to me, "My grace is sufficient for you, for my power is made perfect in weakness." Therefore I will boast all the more gladly about my weaknesses, so that Christ's power may rest on me. That is why, for Christ's sake, I delight in weaknesses, in insults, in hardships, in persecutions, in difficulties. For when I am weak, then I am strong. (NIV)

Each time he said, "My grace is all you need. My power works best in weakness." So now I am glad to boast about my weaknesses, so that the power of Christ can work through me. That's why I take pleasure in my weaknesses, and in the insults, hardships, persecutions, and troubles that I suffer for Christ. For when I am weak, then I am strong. (NLT)

INK

Are you a photographer? Create a gallery of photos that show God's vast power: the wide-open sky, the crashing ocean, powerful waterfalls, towering mountain ranges. Reminders such as these help us understand our smallness in view of God's bigness.

DAY FOUR

THINK

Examine each of these metaphors that God uses for us. Write down what each tells us about our weakness and God's strength:

- We are clay and God is the potter.

- We are sheep and God is the shepherd.

- We are children and he is the heavenly Father.

- We are servants and he is the Master.

LINK

Pick one of the passages above, grab a friend, and work together to memorize it this week.

INK

Do you know what a *faith marker* is? Old Testament characters would sometimes use physical markers such as rocks or monuments to commemorate the work of God in their lives. The same thing can remind you today of God's great strength in your life.

Find a natural marker such as a large, smooth rock or a branch from a tree. Using paint or permanent markers, write on your object a reminder of what God has done. You could write something like *God rescued me from* _____; or *When I was* ____, *God was* _____. Date it and place it prominently in your room, car, yard, or family meeting place.

DAY FIVE

THINK

Okay. You're getting the idea that you need to let go. But how? You've got 20 things to do today, people are depending on you, and you just have to hold on.

- **Prayer is constant.**
- **Prayer is relational.**
- **Prayer is intimate.**
- **Prayer is life changing.**

The Bible teaches that we are designed for quiet stillness as much as we are designed for action. One of the first ways you can begin to let go is through prayer. Prayer is an act of speaking and listening. It's conversation—whenever and wherever. It is not to be pulled out at dinner and youth group and bedtime, and then put away until the next assigned time.

Respond to these prompts:
In the past week, I have prayed during the following times in the following places:

These are the things I have prayed for:

I would estimate my total number of "prayer minutes" might be:

Wait! Do you see a problem with this survey? It makes prayer into a checklist—not the intimate, steady communication of a daily relationship. What does prayer look like in your life? If you haven't spent much time praying before, how could you incorporate prayer naturally into your day?

LINK

Find an adult who has a growing, dynamic prayer life. If you can't think of anyone, talk to your youth leader or a Christian friend to see if he or she can point you to someone.

Once you find a powerful pray-er, ask these questions:

- How is prayer less like a ritual for you and more like a daily conversation?
- When do you find time to pray?
- What are some practical ways you create stillness in your daily life?

INK

Try journaling your prayers.

Keeping a prayer journal is not about trying to impress God so he'll answer a request. It's about keeping a record of the amazing stuff he's done. Some people use their prayer journals to record requests and answers; others use it to meditate on certain verses and "pray them back" to God.

Another method is journaling "picture prayers" where symbols and doodles create reminders of God's promises. What does a picture prayer look like? Stick figures or other simple pictures can be wrapped in words, like *God protects me*. Or the words *God's grace* could form an umbrella. Scripture references can form links in a larger chain. Imagine the possibilities!

DIGGING DEEPER

Read some of these passages about prayer, and then write your own definition of prayer based on the Bible's teachings:

- Matthew 6:5
- Luke 11:1–13
- Acts 4:24
- Ephesians 6:18

Using words or pictures, take a minute and write down prayers of thanksgiving, requests, or praises to God.

DAY SIX

THINK

As you think further about giving up control and relying on Christ, read what Brent Curtis has to say:

> When we hear the phrase "trust totally in God," most of us probably sigh, hearing it as one more requirement that we can't live up to. But what if we were to listen to our hearts, and hear it as a need to lay down our "doings" and simply make our needs known to Christ, and rest in Him? [6]

Rest. It's definitely a choice. An attitude we take toward life's challenges. The world says we can do this if we just "think positively" about our problems. But if you're a follower of the living God, you know it takes something more than optimism. It takes Spirit living.

Spirit living is not a weird, mystical force. It is realizing that something outside you is giving you daily strength and encouragement. It is knowing that God has your back at all times. It is more than willpower. When the Holy Spirit camps out in your very soul, your attitude toward life is bound to change.

Let's say you tried out for a sports team for two years in a row, but still didn't make it. Positive thinking might lead you to say, "Hey, I'm better than all those jerks anyway; I'm a great player—that coach doesn't know what he's missing!" But Spirit living leads you to realize that God knows what's best for you; you can move forward with confidence that God is preparing you for something better.

Think of a challenging situation in your life right now.

How would a "positive thinker" respond to your experience? How can Spirit living help you approach your situation? Write about the different responses here.

Situation in My Life

Positive-Thinking Approach

Spirit-Living Approach

LINK

In 1986, an award-winning movie called *The Mission* was released. Instead of watching the latest big-screen flick with your friends this weekend, gather up your family and watch this powerful story about a missionary's efforts to bring God's love to South America.

Two of the characters—one played by Robert De Niro and the other by Jeremy Irons—illustrate two different ways of approaching ministry. One relies on his own power, and the other relies on God's leading. With which do you find it easiest to identify?

> **WARNING:**
>
> This movie has moments of violence. It's not a fluffy, feel-good piece of entertainment. Your mom or dad can check out pluggedinonline.com to help decide if it's right for your family.

INK

Poetry isn't just food for dorks, crazy people, deep thinkers, or dead writers. Poetry is heart-pounding music, pieces of truth ground up into small bites, or huge emotions painted with words. Writing poetry can give you a place to take unspoken things and give them form.

As the week comes to an end, what's in your heart? If you don't know how to start a poem, try to write a simple honest sentence such as, *"I believe God is . . ."* or ask a question like *"Why do I always . . . ?"*

Poetry is one way to record your journey—a story that needs to be told!

WEEK FOUR: GETTING STARTED

WHAT IS MY FOOTHOLD?

Like a straight-up slab of red sandstone, the footholds the world offers come in all shapes and sizes, but none of them provide much stability. This week's video revealed that both girls and guys look for self-worth in their public image, but it's not a secure foundation.

What is your anchor, your foothold in life? Clinging desperately to the side of life's mountain, girls grasp at fragile beauty, and guys pray that their physical strength will hold out. We scrape and claw at the vertical face of our lives, but we can't figure out why we start to slide.

So where can you place all your weight when you're hoisting yourself up to the next level? There's only one spot sturdy enough to anchor you, and that spot is God himself. He defines who you are, manufactures the best equipment to get you to the top, and gives your wobbly limbs strength when they start to shake. Climb on!

My action plan for this week is . . .

DAY ONE

THINK

Who do you think you are?

In the wrong tone of voice, that question sounds rude. But for today, it's a great starting point. You need to honestly ask yourself who you think you are.

Circle all the nouns you would use to describe yourself and then add some of your own.

Name: _____

Age: _____

controller	rebel	follower	intellectual
musician	complainer	pessimist	thinker
optimist	brother	crybaby	diva
son	athlete	reader	fashion queen
sister	skeptic	gamer	soccer player
friend	organizer	singer	victim
daughter	leader	encourager	animal lover
debater	nerd	bookworm	swimmer
music lover	cousin	introvert	flirt

Who do other people say you are?

Go back to that same list and underline the labels you think other people would give you. **Are they the same? If not, how come? Explain your answer.**

LINK

It's one thing to be hurt by others' false perceptions; it's quite another to inflict the same pain on someone else. Pull away from self-mode for a second and read Rick Warren's take on how we can—but shouldn't—destroy each other with unfair judgments:

> During the Cold War, both sides agreed that some weapons were so destructive they should never be used. Today chemical and biological weapons are banned, and the stockpiles of nuclear weapons are being reduced and destroyed. For the sake of fellowship, you must destroy your arsenal of relational nuclear weapons, including condemning, belittling, comparing, labeling, insulting, condescending, and being sarcastic.[7]

Define these words:

Condemning:

Condescending:

Sarcastic:

Does this passage convict you about someone you've treated poorly? Pick up the phone and ask that person for forgiveness. While that's incredibly hard to do, great restoration can occur when people humble themselves and ask forgiveness. Don't do it to bring attention to yourself—otherwise, it's an insincere contradiction. Do it because it's the right thing. Someone's heart may begin to heal because of your obedience.

INK

Sometimes writing a letter is an easier way to apologize and ask for forgiveness. If making that phone call gives you a sick feeling in your stomach, write a note of repentance. Then deliver it! Restoration of a relationship is worth it!

DAY TWO

THINK

What does God say about you?

Read this bit of Psalm 139 from the NIV and find out . . .

O LORD, you have searched me and you know me.

You know when I sit and when I rise; you perceive my thoughts from afar.

You discern my going out and my lying down; you are familiar with all my ways.

Before a word is on my tongue you know it completely, O LORD.

You hem me in—behind and before; you have laid your hand upon me.

Such knowledge is too wonderful for me, too lofty for me to attain.

Where can I go from your Spirit? Where can I flee from your presence?

If I go up to the heavens, you are there; if I make my bed in the depths, you are there.

If I rise on the wings of the dawn, if I settle on the far side of the sea,

even there your hand will guide me, your right hand will hold me fast.

If I say, "Surely the darkness will hide me and the light become night around me,"

even the darkness will not be dark to you; the night will shine like the day, for darkness is as light to you.

For you created my inmost being; you knit me together in my mother's womb.

I praise you because I am fearfully and wonderfully made; your works are wonderful, I know that full well.

My frame was not hidden from you when I was made in the secret place. When I was woven together in the depths of the earth, your eyes saw my unformed body. All the days ordained for me were written in your book before one of them came to be.

Now read the Psalm out loud again, but this time replace the words *me* and *my* with your name.

LINK

If you find that your worldly identity is competing with your true identity in Christ, you can be sure your friends are struggling too. Write a letter to a friend who may be having a difficult time accepting what God says about his or her value. You might even personalize Psalm 139 by inserting your friend's name and include a copy of that Psalm in your letter as an encouragement.

DIGGING DEEPER

An outstanding book on the topic of our identity in Christ is Giglio's *I Am Not But I Know I AM*. Take a look at it!

INK

You know those magazine collages you used to make in elementary school? Try a new twist by creating an identity collage of digital images, words, and phrases. Use it for the cover of your binder at school or a poster for your room. If you're not really into this kind of art, try using bumper stickers. Find words that identify you with Christ—rather than with the world.

DAY THREE

THINK

These aren't only teen questions; they are human questions.

What do others think of me?

I DON'T WANT TO BE LAME OR DORKY.

Why do I get nervous in social situations?

DOES ANYONE ACCEPT THE REAL ME?

DIGGING DEEPER

Read these words from Brennan Manning and ponder the questions that follow:

> The Kingdom belongs to people who aren't trying to look good or impress anybody, even themselves. They are not plotting how they can call attention to themselves, worrying about how their actions will be interpreted or wondering if they will get gold stars for their behavior. . . . The child doesn't have to struggle to get himself in a good position for having a relationship with God; he doesn't have to create a pretty face for himself. All he has to do is happily accept the cookies: the gift of the Kingdom.[8]

Why do you think it's so hard to ignore the opinions of our peers?

What are some strategies to keep out all of the false voices and the world's shallow opinions?

LINK

You haven't been a kid for a while now, but sometimes children's stories—especially the deep ones—have great value for us older folks. If you can, get a copy of Max Lucado's animated video *You Are Special*. (If you can't find the video, there's a picture book by the same title that's worth checking out.) It tells the story of a puppet that isn't as perfect or handsome as his friends. But he learns to find his real value by going to visit the Puppet Maker. Retreat back to childhood, pop some popcorn, and watch this parable with a friend.

INK

Sometimes it's good to sweep out your emotional closet. On a blank piece of paper, write down all the memories of painful things people have said to your face, implied by their behavior, or even whispered behind your back.

It won't feel good! But once you've written them down, ask one of your parents or a trusted mentor to pray with you as you hold that sheet of paper: *Please, God, remove those sad memories and heal the wounds. Replace these lies with the truth. Help me to forgive those who have hurt me.*

Don't write down the memories here—because when you're finished the two of you need to get rid of the evidence! Burn it (carefully), destroy it, soak it in water, throw it over a cliff, or let the dog eat it! Okay, maybe not that last one—it would be bad for the dog—but you get the point!

DAY FOUR

THINK

Do you think the *Ultimate Choice* cast members altered their behavior a little bit once the cameras started rolling? I'm sure if they were honest, they would admit that everything changes when you're in the spotlight. Self-consciousness kicks in. Gestures become more deliberate. The cool factor takes over. We've all been there.

Imagine if your life were like the Olympic Games. You're an athlete and your performance is being assessed by a set of judges. Write in the number from 1–10 (10 is a perfect score) that each of your "life judges" might give you.

My Teacher: _____   My Parents' Friends: _____

My Dad: _____   Kids at School: _____

My Best Friend: _____   My Girlfriend/Boyfriend/Crush: _____

My Youth Pastor: _____   A Perfect Stranger: _____

My Mother: _____

Aren't you glad that your life's success isn't dependent on the scores from a set of judges? Even so, we act as though pleasing other people is the most important pursuit in the world. Think of roles you've played the past few years. Be honest with yourself. What were those roles and whom were you trying to please?

Example: I tried to become *more athletic* in order to please/impress *the girls in my PE class*.

I tried to become _____ in order to please/impress

_____.

I tried to become _____ in order to please/impress

_____.

I tried to become _____ in order to please/impress

_____.

LINK

Make two index cards—one for you and one for a friend. This week, memorize this verse together:

> It's in Christ that we find out who we are and what we are living for. Long before we first heard of Christ and got our hopes up, he had his eye on us, had designs on us for glorious living, part of the overall purpose he is working out in everything and everyone. —Ephesians 1:11

INK

Create an outline of a person with nothing but empty space inside. (Make it as big or small as you'd like.) Fill in all the empty space with words and phrases that identify you as one of Christ's children. Or, find a photograph of yourself and tape it below. Then write words and phrases around the picture.

If you're an artist, try changing the style and shape of the words, making some bigger and others smaller. Place them in strategic spots, such as writing "running God's race" inside one of the legs or "compassionate friend" near the heart.

Here are some words and phrases you might use to decorate your "human graphic."

God's child

mighty warrior

AMBASSADOR

reader of the Word

forgiven

blessed

ACCEPTED

UNDER GOD'S WARRANTY

heaven bound

peacemaker

servant

Christ follower

DAY FIVE

THINK

The *Ultimate Choice* rock-climbing event required endurance and strength, and many admired Tish for her physical and mental perseverance. Our culture often promotes performance as the ultimate goal, but is there ever a time when we might have it backward?

Do it now. Make those good grades. Clean your room. Get it right. Be strong and don't quit. Grow up already! Succeed! Can't you do it any faster?

Whew. How can you possibly survive this kind of pressure?

Does the Bible always tell us to perform faster and better?

When was the last time you rested in God's presence doing absolutely nothing?

Write down the top three pressures you're feeling right now. Who is pushing you to succeed?

If you failed at any one of these three things, would God's opinion of you change at all?

LINK

Too many pressures swirling around your head? Ask your mom or dad to take you somewhere for an afternoon, or even a weekend—a quiet seaside town, a hike through some pine trees, maybe even a meadow outside of town at midnight. Talk with one another about the big world, the one where you aren't the star player.

Be still. Listen to your heartbeat and observe the grandeur of God.

INK

Download a digital photo of a rock climber on the face of a cliff or mountain such as Half Dome in Yosemite National Park or scaling the red rocks in Utah or Sedona. Design a wallpaper for your computer by superimposing the words of Psalm 18:2 NIV on the photo as a reminder of your life's foothold.

The LORD is my rock, my fortress and my deliverer; my God is my rock, in whom I take refuge.

DAY SIX

THINK

In Western culture, we're all about confidence and self-promotion. Football players slip in their celebratory dances in the end zone, rappers wear their attitudes on their sleeves, and celebrities accept awards on TV every night of the week.

It's no wonder that humility is considered a no-no in our competitive world. We've been taught how to self-promote and hide our weaknesses, but few of us have much training in disappointment or inadequacy. On *Ultimate Choice*, Whitney's confidence was shattered when she didn't climb the wall very well. What are *we* to do when our grand achievements don't materialize?

Like many of God's upside-down plans, he has designed a way for us to have both humility and confidence.

Spread across the surface of this big teeter-totter, write down different areas in which you are either very strong, very weak, or somewhere in the middle.

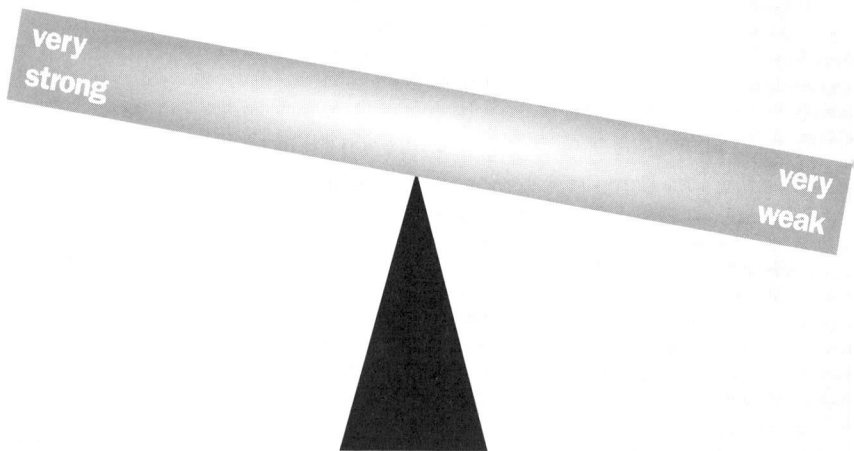

What is your confidence or insecurity based on? (Past experience, other people's observations, personal achievement or failure, etc.)

Why is it important to have your inner confidence shaped by God's opinion rather than your own successes?

LINK

Ask a parent, youth pastor, or other adult about a time when they experienced a huge failure. Maybe they were fired from a job, blew it for a sports team, crumbled under pressure, or maybe even experienced a divorce.

Write down three to five questions for them to answer about that experience. Discuss the life lessons they were able to learn and how they persevered in spite of their failure.

INK

Songs like R. Kelly's "I Believe I Can Fly," Christina Aguilera's "Beautiful," or Mariah Carey's "Hero" seem like great self-esteem boosters on the surface. But are they really?

Most of the motivational messages we hear in schools, from celebrities, or on therapy talk shows tell us we only have ourselves to depend on. Compare these flimsy answers with the much deeper message of Casting Crowns' song "Who Am I?" In it, the songwriter echoes the Bible's truth about our real value.

> *Who am I, that the Lord of all the earth*
> *Would care to know my name*
> *Would care to feel my hurt?*
> *Who am I, that the Bright and Morning Star*
> *Would choose to light the way*
> *For my ever wandering heart?*
>
> *Not because of who I am*
> *But because of what You've done*
> *Not because of what I've done*
> *But because of who You are . . .*[9]

Are you a musician? Write a song that explores the theme of our identity in Christ. Like David in the Psalms, you will be able to use music to express a profound truth.

HOW CAN GOD TRANSFORM MY FAILURES?

It seems in every reality show, every sporting event, and every life story, we are told to suppress weakness and glorify success. Jason, DJ, and Jeremiah all shared in this week's *Ultimate Choice* episode about the frustration of blunders and missteps. Donovan and Alicia have struggled with the more serious implications of alcohol and eating disorders. Perhaps you have dealt with deep issues of personal failure and disappointment.

The Bible is full of broken people. God's people are often weak and their lives cluttered with an untidy mess of sin and failure. But as we discovered in Week Three, such failure is often the time for God to make his grandest entrance. How can God be glorified—even when we get it all wrong?

My action plan for this week is . . .

DAY ONE

THINK

At some point, you've faced a moment of awareness, a time when you finally said a-ha!—an experience that forced you to confront a deep truth. Have you ever experienced something that made you very aware of your weakness? Perhaps you recognized that you were repeating the same mistakes over and over again. Maybe you realized that you weren't the "perfect" child your parents were expecting. Maybe your hopes and dreams for success melted under the heat of personal failure.

Many of the cast members of *Ultimate Choice* didn't confront their weaknesses until they were a little older, and some people avoid such confrontations altogether. But maybe you're a little further along in recognizing your own struggles.

Describe a time in your life when you recognized your imperfections. What happened to make you aware? How did you feel when you experienced defeat?

LINK

Do you know someone who, at least in your mind, seems perfect? Maybe it's a Christian friend, a youth leader, or a teacher. The truth is that what appears on the outside isn't always an accurate picture.

What do you assume is true about this person's "perfect" life?

Okay, now let's test the illusion. Get together with this person and share your perceptions. (Be wise in what you say—the point of this is not to make the person feel guilty.) After he or she has had a chance to hear your version, ask the person to share some of the hidden truths about his or her personal journey. **What weaknesses have they had to overcome? What disappointments and failures paved the way for God to be glorified? How was your "illusion of perfection" corrected by their honesty?**

INK

Remember the "faith markers" from Week Three? Consider another way to use a faith marker to remind yourself of God's strength when you are weak.

Attach a symbol to a leather cord or string to wear as a necklace. Some people find that a daily reminder of their reliance on Jesus Christ is both a personal comfort and an outward testimony. Crosses are universal, but perhaps your life might trigger something unique. An old key might represent God's "open door;" a nail can represent Christ's sacrificial suffering; a gold ring can be a sign of faithfulness. Whatever symbol you choose, it can be both a public or private reminder of your personal walk with God.

DAY TWO

THINK

If failure isn't an option, then neither is God's redemption.

Just like the classic physics lesson, the same is true for our lives: For every action there is an equal and opposite reaction. Fortunately for us, the greater our failure, the greater God's forgiveness. God is able to take our sin and failure and transform it into something new. You heard Jeremiah wisely affirm on the video, "I may have failed for this moment, but I'm not going to fail overall!"

Using Newton's law, see if you can explore the ways that God has countered your failures with his goodness. Maybe use this sentence as your starting point for each one: *When I was . . . . God turned it into . . .*

LINK

Do you know someone who uses sign language? Some of the most beautiful signs are those that visually represent God's love and redemption for us. Signing is not only beneficial for the deaf, certain signs can also be symbols for our relationship with Jesus Christ.

Try to learn the signs for some of your favorite worship songs. Ask someone who knows sign language how to communicate words like *forgiveness, salvation, cleanse,* and *relationship*. What do they communicate about the love of God? (If you don't know anyone who knows sign language, check the Internet. There are numerous online sign language dictionaries.)

INK

One of the most dramatic stories in the New Testament is the conversion of Saul. The transformation was so complete that even his name changed to Paul! With the help of your friends, write a script for your youth group or children's ministry that dramatizes this powerful story. You can also look online for great downloadable skits and plays from dozens of Christian drama sites.

DAY THREE

THINK

You may have grown up thinking that churches were only filled with God-fearing, morally upstanding adults. By now, you've probably figured out that your impressions were incorrect!

Your small group might have explored the truth about sin this week: *All of us are included in the sin equation—not just "bad" folks.* **Have you been surprised by others' failures at times—especially from people whose lives were supposed to be holy? Does growing up in church keep us from being part of the "sinners club"? What do you think?**

Sometimes we use other people's faults to our own advantage. Here are a few ways:

- We use others' weakness to make us feel better about ourselves.
- We use others' weakness as a source of gossip or entertainment.
- We use others' weakness to create a lower standard for our own behavior. *("But I'm so much better than that person is!")*

Write about a time when you were tempted to act in one of these ways. What would be more God-honoring ways to respond to others' failures?

LINK

Alicia and Jesse shared their admiration for what the other cast members had accomplished. This isn't typical of most young people's reactions. Too often, we secretly harbor jealousy and resentment toward someone else when he or she conquers an obstacle or finds great success.

Have you heard of a friend's recent success? Perhaps he or she has overcome a difficult trial, accomplished something big, or maybe matured over the past several months. Don't hide your admiration out of jealousy! Share your enthusiasm for what has happened! Write a letter or make a phone call right away and encourage your friend or family member to keep moving forward.

INK

With the accessibility of technology today, more and more people are producing amateur videos with great results. If you have some background in video production, consider making a music video or short film that illustrates how we tend to judge ourselves—not by what God says about us—but by how we compare others to ourselves. Ask your youth leader if you can share it at the next meeting.

DAY FOUR

THINK

One of the greatest by-products of failure is often the most overlooked. To know that we have failed—utterly and completely—is to know what someone else has gone through. Think of how many times the group in the video learned humility through their own failures. **It's been said that a person cannot have both innocence and compassion at the same time. What do you think this means?**

Make a list of difficult things that have happened in your life. What kind of support can you now give others because of those experiences? What did you learn that you could now share with someone going through a similar trial?

LINK

Your sins and weaknesses are not merely black marks in the grade book of your life. These same "failing grades" can be transformed by God into life-giving resources you can eventually share with others.

If you have access to a peer-counseling program at school—or you know of a brother, sister, or friend who is on the brink of failure himself—don't just stand by and watch! You've been there before. You understand the particular pain associated with his or her trial. Get involved in the process of intervention and recovery. Others just like you need support and compassion.

INK

We've talked about poetry before . . . how it takes big emotions and places them in words that can almost be *seen* and *touched* rather than just *felt*. Think about the Psalms of David for a moment. Many of them are "failure poems"—song lyrics and poetry that bring all of his sadness into sharp focus before God.

How do you start a "failure poem"? Try starting with a single word that captures your emotion, like *devastation* or *inadequacy* and then describe what it feels like. But don't leave it there! Follow up all that honest emotion with the truth of God's promises. A second verse or stanza might start with a word like *peace* or *rescue*. Your poem just might capture what God has done for you in a way that can bring comfort to others.

DAY FIVE

THINK

Okay. We've established that failure and sin are part of the human condition. But am I doomed to repeat my mistakes? What happens if I keep sinning over and over? Does God really promise that I can be victorious over sin and live a life of holiness?

In the video, Tish defines failure as "something going wrong and you not doing anything about it." Jason shared that when he looked at his life, he didn't like what he saw. While most teenagers would blame others or circumstances to justify their bad behavior, we need to recognize God's requirement for repentance and change. **Do you think most people can just wake up one morning and turn it all around on their own? What do you think is required for someone to change?**

LINK

The "fruit of the spirit" is the God-given evidence that we are actually his children. But fruit doesn't emerge full-grown and ripened in a few hours or several days. Fruit matures slowly, and so will you.

As you grow in Christ, you need to make yourself open to your parents, pastors, Christian friends, and church community. Ask yourself these relational questions:

- Am I surrounding myself with a mature community of believers in Jesus Christ?
- Do I have a mentor I can depend on when I am faced with difficult temptations?
- Are my closest friends the ones who will pull me back in—or encourage me to pursue my selfish whims?

Will you fall from the tightrope in the months and years to come? You bet. Your relational safety net needs to be wide, strong, and flexible in order to cushion the concrete below.

INK

If you can, get a copy of Jadon Lavik's song "What If" from the album *Life on the Inside*. The lyrics ask the penetrating question of whether God's love is dependent on either our success or failure.

His song is a powerful restatement of Romans 8:37–38:

> *None of this fazes us because Jesus loves us. I'm absolutely convinced that nothing—nothing living or dead, angelic or demonic, today or tomorrow, high or low, thinkable or unthinkable—absolutely nothing can get between us and God's love because of the way that Jesus our Master has embraced us.*

DAY SIX

THINK

Your journey is just beginning.

Your *UltimateStory* has been written lovingly by God's hand, and you are living it out every day in your school, home, and community. You may not be jumping out of airplanes or crashing through white water, but your challenges are no less dramatic and are just as exhilarating.

As a disciple of Christ, you are equipped with everything you need to make your journey count. Read this passage from "The Agony of Defeat" by J. Hampton Keathley:

> *Because of a workaholic mentality, an activity-oriented bent or a desire to get things done and to be successful, there is the tendency to rush ahead without taking time with the Lord to draw near to Him and His resources and to put on the full armor of God. Such is not only unwise, but it often causes us to be insensitive to serious failures in our own lives and ministries, which grieve and quench the Spirit, and leave us defenseless against the enemy because we are then operating in our own strength and wisdom. Ultimately, then, these failures stand in the way of our progress and ability to handle the various challenges in life.*[10]

What do you think is the "full armor of God"? How can you draw near to God in specific ways?

LINK

Have you ever heard of a life map? They can take many forms. Some people try to set out goals and dreams on paper, while others see personal diaries or journals as another way to "map out" their lives.

During this week, consider creating an actual map of your life. Instead of using paragraphs or diary entries, you can actually create a visual "atlas" of your life and its beautiful, complex story.

Symbols	What They Might Represent
	Shapes of buildings, houses, etc., with words in them; outlines of states or countries—Places you've lived or important locations.
	Roads, trails, rocky paths, or straight highways—Directions you've headed, different paths you've taken in life.
	Dark clouds, storms, tornadoes, or earthquakes—Obstacles you've encountered in your life, such as divorce, depression, illness, or difficulty.
	Boulders, brick walls, fences, or gates—Sin patterns that have held you back, made you stumble, or tripped you up.
	Sunshine, open highways, hospitals, or rescue teams—Places where God brought strength, forgiveness, or restoration to your life.

Start with a *big* sheet of paper and establish a starting point—your birth. Then, using symbols, words, and pictures, begin to mark the life moments where God intervened on your behalf.

On the left are some ideas for map symbols.

A map like this is a powerful reminder of what God has done in your life—and it's never finished! You can leave plenty of open spaces as God continues to direct your life story.

BRINK

The first of your Ultimate Choices is over—you've finished five weeks of examining your life and your faith. But now you're poised at the brink. What are you going to do from here? You've spent five weeks challenging yourself and making choices—is it all going to stop here, on the last page of this book? Or will you continue to live in a way that makes a difference? That's your next choice.

DIGGING DEEPER

- When Moses spoke to the people of Israel before they faced a hostile enemy, he told them, *"The LORD will fight for you; you need only to be still"* (**Exodus 14:14** NIV).

- David shared this request during a frantic time: *"I'm asking GOD for one thing, only one thing: To live with him in his house my whole life long. I'll contemplate his beauty; I'll study at his feet. That's the only quiet, secure place in a noisy world . . ."* (**Psalm 27:4–5**).

- Consider this instruction: *"Quiet down before GOD, be prayerful before him. Don't bother with those who climb the ladder, who elbow their way to the top"* (**Psalm 37:7**).

- Look at what Jesus shared during one of his sermons: *"Here's what I want you to do: Find a quiet, secluded place so you won't be tempted to role-play before God. Just be there as simply and honestly as you can manage. The focus will shift from you to God, and you will begin to sense his grace"* (**Matthew 6:6**).

PERSONAL NOTES

PERSONAL NOTES

ENDNOTES

1. Eugene Peterson, *The Message Remix: The Bible in Contemporary Language* (Colorado Springs: NavPress 2003), 897–898.

2. Norman L Geisler and Frank Turek, *I Don't Have Enough Faith to Be an Atheist* (Wheaton, IL: Crossway Books 2004), 24.

3. Rick Warren, *The Purpose-Driven Life* (Grand Rapids: Zondervan 2002), 79.

4. Brennan Manning, *The Ragamuffin Gospel* (Sisters, OR: Multnomah 2005), 202

5. Louie Giglio, *I Am Not But I Know I AM* (Sisters, OR: Multnomah 2004), 29.

6. Brent Curtis and John Eldredge, *The Sacred Romance* (Nashville: Thomas Nelson 2001), 170–171.

7. Warren, *The Purpose-Driven Life*, 157.

8. Manning, *The Ragamuffin Gospel*, 53.

9. Casting Crowns, "Who Am I?" *Casting Crowns*, Reunion, 2003.

10. J. Hampton Keathley, "The Agony of Defeat," *Bible.org*, 2006, <http://www.bible.org/page.asp?page_id=983>.